All rights reserved by US copyright laws. No portions of this book can be used without the express permission of the copyright holder.

Copyright – Marta Moran Bishop

Copyright – Saket Suryesh

A Walk
Through Nature

© 2013 Marta Moran Bishop

Crowe Press

Saket Suryesh © 2013

Cover Art by R. Jade Lazlow

A Walk Through Nature

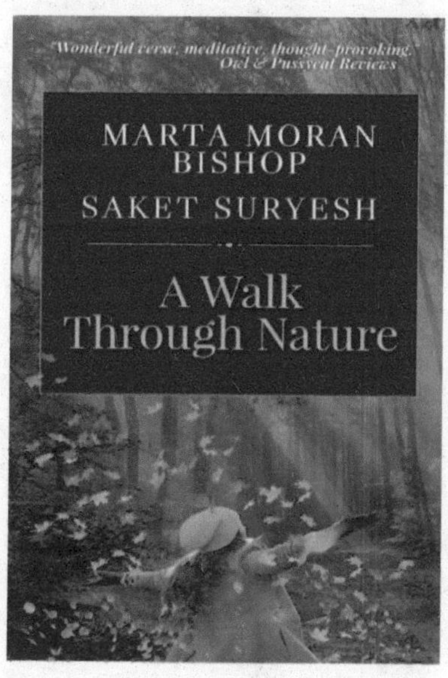

Marta Moran Bishop
Poetry and Saket Suryesh
Cover Art R. Jade Lazlo

THE TREE

Brightly the sun covers the leaves,
Turning them from green to gold.

Feeding the tree health and life,
Giving it the strength to bloom.

A place for the birds to sit,
For the bugs to crawl and feed.

A place of shelter for squirrels,
And horses and humans too.

How bleak the world with no tree,
No green boughs to sit under.

None to whisper to the wind,
As leaves rustle and birds sing.

I WEPT FOR THE TREE

I wept for the tree as it died
For the lives lost too young
The mistakes I have made
The chances not taken
With each seasonal change
I grow and learn
Spreading my wings
To the sky and beyond
I will stumble again
And pick myself up
See the beauty around
And find joy in the tree

AUTUMNS BRILLIANT FINERY

Majestically the trees are dressed
In autumns brilliant finery
Their colors brightly light the way
Leaves of red, orange, and gold
Breathtaking beauty warms our souls
Before winters chill sets in.

THE HAWK

Above the trees, sailing through the clouds
Over the rainbow flew the hawk
On the flowing breezes, wings spread wide
Gliding, watching, his young to feed
Dancing through fair winds he flew
On and on he circled until
On the chimney with grace he landed
Regally sitting, talons clinging
Glorious wings spread wide to dry
Then with a screech he flew again
To ride the wind, dance among the clouds
Gliding, watching young to feed

CHROME

Across the field they ran
And through the trees they flew
Up the hill they scampered
Over the river they jumped
Regal is her fur friend
Majestically he moves
Long legs and golden mane
And tail that flows behind
His silver eyelashes
Frame loving brown eyes
Speaking volumes to her
Of a lifetime together
Continuously friends
And forever family

DARK SHADY PLACES

I love the forest with its dark shady paths
Sunlight filtering down through branches and
leaves
Squirrels and chipmunks scampering all
around
Quiet and peaceful away from the noise
Of mankind's chatter, hammers, and car horns

Nature around me abounding with life
Listening to sounds of the birds and crickets
The play of water rushing over rocks
Glimmering sunlight catching the whitecaps

A fox peeking at me through leaves and brush
Off in the distance a shy little deer
With a majestic buck with wings on its feet
Owl hooting the last goodbye as dawn breaks

All of nature's beauty quiets my thoughts
Seeping deep into my heart and soul
Filling all of me with a natural peace
Mysterious glory seeking my soul
Making me one with the trees and sunlight
As I walk along this dark, shady path
I am filled with the sound of life and love
The essence of life is in these woods

If you walk quietly and allow it in
You too can be filled with its brimming light
We all think it is death we fear
But its living we're afraid of
To ride the wind across the sky
And sail our ship through rough waters
The breezes blowing through our hair

And the sand between our toes
Horses' mane whipping in our face
Legs wrapped around and arms out wide
Laughing, singing, feeling, living

I wouldn't want to go back in time
I wouldn't wish to do it over
I like the place I am at right now
I like where my heart and soul reside
But it would be nice to wipe away
Lines of laughter and sorrow that rest
Upon my face and look thirty again
Alas, I am forever stuck with them
So instead of wishing them all gone
I'll rejoice in the stories they tell

FINDING THE LIGHT

Across the years my mind flies
Through muddy passages
My heart must find its own way
To shed light in those places
Where emptiness lives

Lost ones living on in caverns
In dark places of my soul
Striving to be remembered
Will breathe air into those flames
Till they are beacons of fire

Throwing sunlight at shadows
Lighting cold spaces with warmth
Uncovering lost dreams and loves
And memories of times past
Bringing the promise of hope

Releasing shackled baggage
Tangled in remembering
Leaving love and knowledge
Of those we have left behind
They will not be forgotten

On wings of bright light and wind
The doors will open wider

Showing us that truth is more
Than we had known before
Long gone are the seeds of doubt

With those memories of loss
That serve only to drag us down
Into the gutter of angst
Hopeless and helpless we feel
Not able to believe it

The end is the beginning
For time ebbs and flows around
In the dance of life it whirls
And we must nurture all we love
With bright light, love, and honor

Cherishing all those embers
To help us remember good
Our lives are not over now
Till all dark spots are gone
And we are free for glory

It is then we will meet again
When the time is ripe for us
With luck are lessons are learned
And we meet again without hurt

Leaving behind old patterns
Become the best we can be

TOGETHER AGAIN AT LAST

Forgotten the dark corners
That followed us through the past
We meet again in splendor
Every meeting a new chance
To learn how to love ourselves
For even those dark spaces
Hold the means to cherish
And accept all that is

DRAGONFLY

Dragonfly oh Dragonfly
Lovely fairy of my heart
Why did you choose to go inside
To a place you could not leave
Was it your time to leave this life
Or did you lose your way

I loved to watch you flying
Over the meadows and fields
Skirting, darting, playing hard
A joyful dance among your friend
But now that summer has ended
And you have moved beyond

Gone over the rainbow bridge
To fly amongst the lilies
And over the grass so green
Darting, dancing, playing still
Your corporal body left behind
And your spirit soaring high

Wind blows through the lonely branches
Autumn has left, winter upon us
Colorful leaves lay on the ground
The tree is closing down, ready for sleep

THE DEATH OF A TREE

We've shared this hill a hundred years and more
Grown from saplings into trees
I'm getting old my friends
Time is catching up
I've branches bare of leaves
The bugs have nested in my trunk
Mankind's salt has eaten into me
Thrown on the winter roads
I thank you for the love you've shared
For the laughter and the tears
I'll stand in your memory
As you finish out your years
For you are the two who became one
And have each other for eternity
My great and loving friends

FRIENDS OR FOES?

Playing chase me bird
In the sky there flew
Hawk with wings of gold
And a black bird too

Shadows high above
Cast darkness below
The two appear friends
But maybe they're foes

THE NURSE MARE

All alone is the mare
With none around who care
No real place to call home

Pulled away from her herd
Not even a jaybird
To keep her all right
On this dark moonlit night

THE TREE

Powerfully the sun shines
On the leaves of green and gold
Bring the tree vigor and life
Give it the strength to blossom

A place for the bugs to crawl
And a shelter for the squirrels
Birds nest in its limbs so high
In tree houses children play

How bleak the world with no tree
No green boughs to sit under
None to whisper to the wind
As leaves rustle and birds sing

RAINBOWS

Sometimes it's a smile
Often just a grin
Then there's a giggle
A chuckle or two

For rainbows are gifts
Forever a light
To give us all joy
Splendor and hope

WINTER

In sunlight's glimmer
Icicles shimmer
The bare branches clothed
Are heavily bowed

Newly fallen snow
The piles do grow
Sparkling all white
They reach such a height

The weather so cold
Is getting real old
Gray days and snow fall
Are losing their pall

THE TWO WHO WERE ONE

Upon the hill, beside the road
Stood two little trees side by side

Over the years they grew as one
Their trunks and branches intertwined

One hundred years and more they stood
Limbs locked in a lovers embrace

Look closely if you want to see
How long these two have grown as one

They lost a friend a year ago
He stood upon the hill near them

One hundred years and more they stood
The two who were one and their friend

Age is showing some limbs dying
Still they hold each other entwined

Their leaves still shade us in the spring
In fall they turn red, orange, and gold

It's in the winter you will see
The hundred years and more they stood

THE YETI SCREAMS IN PURE DELIGHT

Winter brings its own kind of life
The Yeti screams in pure delight

The mountains talk, the glaciers walk
The hunters' prowl and the wolves' growl

The hawks fly and the eagles soar
The woods are dark and terror reigns

Over the plains, above the hills
The cold wind howls and snow grows deep

The Yeti screams in pure delight
Wolves' prowl, hawks fly, and eagles soar

THE DANCE

We'll dance amongst the stars tonight.
Weave webs of shimmering light
Across the clouds our feet will fly
Tripping the light fantastic

Singing our songs of hope and love
Our voices filling the air
Silver notes of glistening sound
Making waves of light and joy.

From star to star we'll weave our web
Gleaming strands of golden net
Leaving behind a trail of light
For those who'll join our dance

SPRING

Light green, bright green, dark green too
Budding leaves upon the trees
Spring has finally come today
Overnight it seems to me

Yesterday the limbs were bare
Just little nubs upon the trees
Now the buds have opened up
Dressed the trees in green again

Sunlight playing in the leaves
Birds all darting in and out
Building nest to house their young
Singing songs of love and play
On the birth of this new day.

WINTER FUN

Breathtakingly it glistens
Branches are laden with snow
Limbs dressed in glimmering white
Cold winds blow through tree and bough

Snow flies as horses frolic
Across the fields they doth zoom
Prancing in the wonderland
Jumping, rolling in their glee.

SLEEP NOW

Shush, go to sleep dear tree
The cold winds are coming

Your leaves have all fallen
Their glory is gone

Dark branches stand starkly
Against the gray sky

Soon the snows will lie deep
Lakes and rivers will freeze

Cold winds will blow strong
Upon your bare limbs

All too soon the warm breeze
Will blow from the south

Again buds will pop out
Upon your long limbs

Rest now lovely tree
While the cold winds blow.

THE DRAGONFLY

On fragile wings of green and blue
Over the field fly one or two
Soaring, dashing above they fly
So beautiful the dragonfly
All summer long they race and dart
At play together they'll not part
Till the cool breeze of fall comes through
And off on wings of green and blue
To warm places goes dragonfly
Beside the lovely butterfly.

The sky has opened up
Released pent up emotions
Healed watered, cleaned
Our earth to it's very soul
Lovely is the autumn rain
Driving down the dust
A full and hearty blast
Before the winters chill

CLOUD PATHS

What manner of creature walks this road
Of silky, fluffy, white
Is it a bridge to nowhere
Or does it lead to a new life

CLOUDS

Clouds flow above the land
On wisps of angel wings
Over us and clear the air
Blue skies abound with promises
Of better days ahead

Gone are the dark and dreary times
When the world was black and gray
And tears poured forth upon the land
Heavily crying
For the list and lonely ones

A brighter future lies ahead
If we can do our part
Keep the earth below us clean
The skies above us bright
Our hearts pure and filled with love
For our brethren wherever they might be

BEAUTY BEYOND

Clouds black and full, fill the sky
With yesterday's poignant memories
Lazily they drift across the heavens
As the sunlight filters through

A rainbow may pop up today
As a further sign from above
That yesterday's rainy day
Can be replaced with fresh delights

To fill our hearts and souls
With the beauty that can be ours
If we can look beyond
And let times gone be forgotten
Then a new day will begin

I love the forest with its dark shady paths
Sunlight filtering down through branches and leaves
Squirrels and chipmunks scampering all around
Quiet and peaceful away from the noise
Of mankind's chatter, hammers, and car horns

Nature around me abounding with life
Listening to sounds of the birds and crickets

The play of water rushing over rocks
Glimmering sunlight catching the whitecaps

A fox peeking at me through leaves and brush
Off in the distance a shy little deer
With a majestic buck with wings on its feet
Owl hooting the last goodbye as dawn breaks

All of nature's beauty quiets my thoughts
Seeping deep into my heart and soul
Filling all of me with a natural peace
Mysterious glory seeking my soul
Making me one with the trees and sunlight

As I walk along this dark, shady path
I am filled with the sound of life and love
The essence of life is in these woods
If you walk quietly and allow it in
You too can be filled with its brimming light
Something there is about the water
Jumping and playing over rocks
As it swiftly moves down toward
The beaver's dam and stops
Frothing, foaming as it hits
A joyful melody

Something there is about the water
That makes you want to smile
Sit and sing a soothing song
And watch the sunlight play
Upon the waves
As they dance across the sandy beach

THE SAILOR

Upon the deck he stands, gray gone from his
head
Hair blonde again, covered by a sailor's cap

Far off in the distance his blue eyes stare
Long gone the haunted look from his
countenance
Forever forward he sails, to new shores he goes

Wind whips through strands of hair uncovered
by his hat
All smiles and hope are his once more
Life begins anew for him, still he loves those his
mortal body left behind

Forever, watching over, holding tight those he
loves
Who will one day start afresh with him, in a new
land beyond these shores

We all think it is death we fear
But its living we're afraid of
To ride the wind across the sky

And sail our ship through rough waters
The breezes blowing through our hair

And the sand between our toes

Horses' mane whipping in our face
Legs wrapped around and arms out wide
Laughing, singing, feeling, living

I wouldn't want to go back in time
I wouldn't wish to do it over
I like the place I am at right now

I like where my heart and soul reside
But it would be nice to wipe away
Lines of laughter and sorrow that rest

Upon my face and look thirty again
Alas, I am forever stuck with them
So instead of wishing them all gone
I'll rejoice in the stories they tell

From Saket Suryesh
An Author and Poet

THE SEARCH FOR ONE SYLLABLE

Sunbeams spread their legs
Lazily on the earth,
A sense of belonging writ on their
Splendid foreheads.
They talk and chatter
As words fall like
Snowflakes to the ground.
Wrap a silence
Around me
A silence which is so eloquent
That it invades my intelligence
With rare violence,
My soul shudders
In the echoes
Of that arrogant feral noise,
Trying helplessly to detect
One syllable which resembles my name.

Fury flows through the boundaries
Words are sharpened to cause the most damage
Love is denied, and threats flow dense in the air.

The pity is that
When threats are common and oft-repeated
They become an option, a possibility,
And love which once danced in divine glory,

Hides its face between
Old wrinkled palms,
Caught between horror and shame.

A heart dies
And peace descends,
A leaf, yellow and dry,
Whispers
People do not die
Because they are given to death
But because they are tired of living,
A difficult love, gasps for its last breath
And stand silent witness
To damned decaying existence of
A dying heart, which had once

Fought with the Gods and sought its guard
Like a Prometheus
And it's white benevolent light
Takes wings and flies into the dark skies.

LOVE AND BETRAYAL

Love sings in a singular voice
And dances on divine music
Betrayal speaks in multiple voices,
And tells different stories,
All of which are true
And lie, at the same time,
Duality of character
Is the basic hue of betrayal,
Like a two edged sword
Which it pierces through
The heart
From which there is no escape.

You can find Saket Suryesh's Books, Stories,
and Poetry
On Amazon.com
And follow him on Facebook, twitter, and
www.saketsuryesh.net

You can find Marta Moran Bishop at www.martamoranbishop.com, & on Facebook, Twitter, Tumblr, and most social media outlets.

www.ingramcontent.com/pod-product-compliance
Lightning Source LLC
La Vergne TN
LVHW030913080826
845145LV00010B/2876

9781939484246